A La Bark Baking

To lorraine, I hope you enjoy baking those for Charlie — but please don't give them to him all at once!

Happy Baking

kris n' charlie
x x x

A La Bark Baking

Over 30 easy, healthy and inexpensive biscuit, treat, meal and cake recipes to make for your dog.

A donation from every book sold will help save homeless greyhounds and lurchers.

Veterinarian approved ingredients.

Kris Owen

Matador
9 Priory Business Park, Wistow Road
Kibworth,
Leicester LE8 0RX, UK
Tel: (+44) 116 279 2299
Email: books@troubador.co.uk
Web: www.troubador.co.uk/matador

ISBN 978-1848762-138

A Cataloguing-in-Publication (CIP) catalogue record for this book
is available from the British Library.

Cover and back photos courtesy of Chris Brignell at www.petographer.co.uk

Typeset in 10pt Arial by Troubador Publishing Ltd, Leicester, UK
Printed in the UK by TJ International, Padstow, Cornwall

Matador is an imprint of Troubador Publishing Ltd

"I have reviewed the list of ingredients and they do not contain any foodstuffs known to be harmful to dogs."

Ruth Humphreys BVet med. CertSAM. MRCVS
Bishops Stortford Veterinary Hospital, Rye Street,
Bishops Stortford, Herts CM23 2HA

www.stortvet.com

Contents

Foreword

Steve Mann
Judge on TV's *Underdog* Show

So, a cook book for dogs eh? Blimey, after years of running Alpha Dog Training School my dogs can't even put on their own oven gloves let alone work a cooker!

Here's the deal; we love our dogs, our dogs love food. What are you waiting for?

Steve (right) judging on the show.

See his dog training site
www.alphadogtrainingschool.co.uk

Introduction

Thank you for purchasing this book: money raised from its sale will help to provide a warm sanctuary for homeless greyhounds and lurchers.

There are so many of them out there, and they really do make the best pet you can ever own... well I am a bit biased as I love the breed!

I would also like to thank my many taste-testing greyhounds and other breeds of dog, which have tirelessly eaten their way through many versions of these recipes to ensure they all pass the 'A La Bark' test.

My thanks also go to my mum and her miniature schnauzer, Archie, for all their home baking and testing.

A big thank you to all of the charities and owners of greys mentioned in the book for their help in sourcing photographs of hounds, as I appreciate how busy they all are.

Why write a cook book for dogs?

It all started as a result of a fun show day in a friend's garden to raise money for local greyhound kennels. The humans were well catered for in the form of a BBQ, but, I quipped, "my dog always scrounges mine! I know what: I'll do dog lunches."

And so it began.

There are quite a few American doggie cook books out there, but many include ingredients not readily sourced in the UK, and some of these cook books also appear to include ingredients that I would not recommend you feed to your dog.

So my aim was to produce simple, quick and healthy recipes that would be fun to make and would be enjoyed by your dog.

If you choose to purchase organic ingredients, so much the better, but this book aims to provide healthy treats for you to bake at home and, organic or not, the choice is yours.

The ingredients should be readily sourced from your local supermarket in the main, or for the few not available I suggest you try a health food shop.

These recipes do not have any added salt or sugar, nor any ingredients that your dog should not have.

Many of the recipes are so easy to make that it is a great way of getting your children or grandchildren involved in caring for their dog. Try baking one of the meatloaves together!

The recipes do not replace your dog's existing diet; they are a fun addition. Please also be aware that if you feed treats to your dog, you should reduce the size of your dog's other meals.

Up to 40% of dogs in the UK may be overweight, which is not good for your dog's health, as just like us, it puts an extra strain on their body. Try some of the low calorie recipes: the dogs still get tasty treats but without piling on the pounds (my hounds love the carrot biscuits).

Ready to start?

I would really recommend that you buy a set of cup measures from your local supermarket: it is the easiest way of baking these recipes, but all measurements are also given in grammes. You can pick up a set of cup measures for only a few pounds, and this avoids the need for scales, extra bowls, etc.

I find that I can do most of these recipes with cup measures and a set of spoons.

I have tried to use ingredients that are easy to source and not too expensive. I often buy meat in the supermarket when it is reduced, and freeze it until I am ready to use it.

Winnie's Apple and Cheddar Muffins (see page 54)

When friends offer me baking apples, I grab them with both hands and make apple sauce. I freeze it in bags of about 2 cups as it keeps for several months.

If I can source wild rabbits I cook them all up in the pressure cooker, bone them and freeze the meat. Again, they keep for months, and the hounds are always happy to have a bit in their dinner.

You can use any shape cookie cutters, but bone shapes are readily available from cake shops online and various online auction sites, and these look fun when you bake for friends' dogs.

One of my current favourite pieces of cooking equipment is silicon loaf and muffin tins. These are great: they require no greasing or lining paper, and the recipes just pop out once cold.

All of the recipes in this book freeze. I usually freeze two-thirds of each batch and keep the rest in an airtight container. The biscuits with real meat in I would recommend storing in the refrigerator.

I hope you have as much fun making these biscuits and treats as I have had in producing this book for you, and that your dog enjoys them too.

Just remember: your dog will love everything you produce, so don't worry if they turn out a funny shape or lumpy: they won't mind – trust me!

Chester's Cheesy Chomps

Light, golden biscuits
The dough is so easy to work with you can make double batches
and freeze some of the biscuits for later.

INGREDIENTS
$^1/_2$ cup (60g) wholemeal flour
1 cup (100g) oats
$1^1/_4$ cups (100g) grated cheese (preferably cheddar)
$^1/_2$ cup (40g) grated parmesan cheese
1 tablespoon olive oil
$^1/_2$ - $^3/_4$ cup (100-150ml) water.

METHOD
Pre heat oven to 180°C gas mark 4.
Cover a baking tray with baking paper.

Mix all of the ingredients except the oil and water together in a large
mixing bowl.

Add the oil and stir with a large spoon.
Add sufficient water to make the dough stick into one ball.
Place onto a floured surface and roll out gently with a floured rolling pin.
Aim to have your dough about ¼ - ½ inch thick.
Cut with a cookie cutter and place onto the baking tray.
Cook in the centre of the oven for 25-30 minutes or until they start to turn slightly golden.
Makes about 24 middle-sized biscuits.

Store in an airtight container; they may keep for weeks, but they will probably be gobbled up long before then!

COOK'S TIP
If you have a good sized food processor, chop your cheese then add all the other dry ingredients. Pulse the processor and add the oil and water slowly. Stop as soon as the dough sticks into one ball. Roll out and cook as normal.

Biscuits made in the processor have a smoother consistency as the oats will have been chopped, but they still taste great.

Chester, a special gentleman and sponsor dog from Greyhound Rescue West of England.

www.grwe.com

Poppy's Sweet Potato and Carrot

Healthy and tasty and a gorgeous colour.

INGREDIENTS
2 cups (260g) wholemeal flour
$^1/_2$ cup (70g) maize flour
1 medium sized sweet potato, peeled
1 large carrot scrubbed
$^1/_2$ cup (70g) sunflower hearts
$^3/_4$ cup (150ml) water
3 tablespoons olive or safflower oil

METHOD
Pre heat oven to 180°C gas mark 4.
Cover a baking tray with baking paper.

In a large bowl, combine the flour and maize flour.

In a food processor finely chop the carrot and potato.

Add the carrots and the potato to the flours and stir well.
Add the sunflower seeds, oil and water and combine into one ball of dough.

If you need to, you can add a little more water.

Turn out onto a floured worktop and knead until well combined and smooth.

Roll out to ½ inch thick and cut out shapes with cookie cutters.
Place onto a baking tray and bake for 30 minutes.

Turn each biscuit over and cook for another 10 minutes, then turn out onto a wire tray to cool.

Makes about 32 middle-sized biscuits.

Poppy the cheeky office girlie at

www.DogsTrust.org.uk

Elly's Elegant Shortbreads

Nice soft biscuits, excellent for little people without too many teeth.

INGREDIENTS
1 cup (130g) wholemeal flour
1 cup (150g) plain flour
1 tablespoon baking powder
125g jar of baby food (shepherds pie
    or other meaty mix with no
    onions or onion powder)
250g lamb mince

METHOD
Pre heat oven to 180°C, gas mark 4.
Cover a baking tray with baking paper.

In a saucepan, or in the microwave, cook the mince in a little water until done. It should take about 10 minutes simmering. Leave to cool.

In a large bowl, combine the flours and baking powder.
Stir in the baby food and drained mince. Combine well with a big spoon.
Add sufficient of the lamb juice to make a dough, it will probably be
$1/2$ cup (100ml).
Turn the dough onto a floured worktop and knead for a few minutes
until smooth. Roll out to $1/4$-$1/2$ inch thick.
Cut with a cookie cutter and place on the baking tray.

Bake for 15 minutes then turn over and continue baking for another
15 minutes.
Makes about 35 middle-sized biscuits.

COOK'S TIP
Another version of this recipe is to replace the meat baby food with
a fisherman's pie variety and add $1/2$ small tin of drained salmon or
tuna in place of the lamb. Milk or water can be used to wet the
dough.

Store these biscuits in the refrigerator as they are not crispy dry.
Excellent biscuits for the more dentally challenged hound, and these
freeze well.

*Miss Elly having a snooze and well
earned retirement, courtesy of*
www.southernlurcherrescue.org.uk

Malarky's Minty Mouthfuls

Not promising miracles – but these herby biscuits can freshen the breath.

INGREDIENTS
1 cup (150g) plain flour
1$^1/_2$ cups (200g) wholemeal flour
$^1/_2$ cup (40g) grated parmesan cheese
1 tablespoon mint
1 tablespoon parsley
1 egg
$^3/_4$ cup milk (150ml)
$^1/_3$ cup olive oil (70ml)

METHOD
Pre heat the oven to 180°C, gas mark 4.
Cover a baking tray with baking paper.

Combine all the dry ingredients in a large bowl.
In a separate bowl, whisk the egg, milk and oil.

Pour the egg mixture into the dry ingredients and stir together with a big spoon.

Use your hands to knead into one ball of dough, then turn onto a floured worktop. Knead for a few minutes until it becomes easier to work with, then roll out to $1/4$-$1/2$ inch thick.

Cut with cookie cutters and place onto the baking tray.

Bake for 20 minutes then turn over and bake for another 10-15 minutes on the other side. They should be starting to turn golden.

COOK'S TIP

If you want crunchier biscuits that last longer, turn the oven off and leave the biscuits in the oven until cool.

Makes about 32 middle-sized biscuits.

Malarky, a rather handsome sponsor and PAT dog, courtesy of ***www.jerseygreyhoundrescue.org.uk/***

Patience Peanut Butter & Banana Bones

These smell gorgeous: just like banana milkshake.

INGREDIENTS
$^1/_4$ cup (77g) unsalted peanut butter
2 peeled bananas as ripe as you like.
$^3/_4$ cup (150ml) soy or rice milk
(or skimmed milk)
$1^1/_2$ cups (200g) wholemeal flour
1 cup (150g) plain flour
1 tablespoon baking powder

METHOD
Pre heat the oven to 180°C, gas mark 4.
Cover a baking tray with baking paper.

Using a hand blender or food processor, blend the peanut butter, bananas and milk until smooth.
Place the flours and baking powder into a separate large bowl.
Add the banana mixture to the flour and stir with a large spoon until it forms a ball of dough.
Turn out onto a floured worktop and knead until smooth.
Use plenty of flour as this dough can be a bit sticky.

Roll out to about $1/4$-$1/2$ inch thick and cut out using a cookie cutter.
Remember these biscuits rise, so err or the slimmer side.
Place the biscuits onto the baking tray.
Cook for 20 minutes, then carefully turn over.

Cook for another 15-20 minutes.

Makes about 34 middle sized biscuits.

COOK'S TIP
These can be made without the baking powder if you don't have any
– they are just fine, just a little thinner.

Patience waiting for her biscuits.
Lovely sponsor dog courtesy of
www.greyhoundsgalore.org.uk/

Princess Peanut Butter & Honey Bones

Very rich, sweet and high in protein but loved by all. Use a smaller cutter for these if you are watching the waistline

INGREDIENTS
2 cups (295g) wholemeal flour
$^{1}/_{2}$ cup (60g) wheatgerm
$^{1}/_{2}$ cup (45g) oats
$^{1}/_{4}$ cup honey
$^{1}/_{2}$ cup (150g) salt free peanut butter
1 cup (200ml) milk
1 egg

METHOD
Pre heat the oven to 180°C gas mark 4.
Cover a baking tray with baking paper.

In a large bowl place the flour, oats and wheatgerm. Stir well.
Add the peanut butter, honey and the egg and stir with a large
spoon.

Add the milk slowly as you may not need it all, dependant upon how
wet your peanut butter is.

With your hands, knead into one ball of dough and then turn out
onto a floured worktop or board.
Knead for a minute or two until smooth and well blended.

Roll out to $1/2$ inch thick and cut with a cutter into biscuits.
Place onto the baking tray and into the oven.

Cook for 15 minutes then carefully turn over and cook for another 15
minutes. They should start to turn golden brown.

Leave to cool on a wire tray.

Makes about 30 middle-sized biscuits.

*Princess, a special girl who
enjoyed her twilight days with
Castledon Kennels Essex.*

www.greyhoundrescueuk.co.uk

Di Loves Liver Biscuits

**Perfect for training, as these are rich and irresistible.
Use a small cutter for these: or a very large one and break into
chunks.**

INGREDIENTS
500g liver (any sort your dog prefers)
3 cups water (600ml)
1 cup (150g) brown rice flour
¹/₄ cup (25g) oats
1 cup (130g) wholemeal flour
1 tablespoon molasses.
2 tablespoons vegetable oil
1 beaten egg

METHOD
Pre heat the oven to 180°C, gas mark 4.
Cover a baking tray with baking paper.
Cook the liver in a saucepan with the water until done (trust me –
don't try this in the microwave).

Allow to cool, then drain the liver and reserve the liquid. Puree the liver in a food processor with just a few spoons of liquid to make it easier for your machine. Add the egg, molasses and oil to the liver puree and blend.

In a large bowl, combine the flours and oats.
Add the liver mixture to the flour and stir until it forms one ball of dough.
Add some of the liver cooking liquid if you need to until the mixture sticks together in one ball.

Turn out onto a floured worktop and knead for a minute or two until well blended. You may need plenty of flour as this is a very sticky dough.
Roll out with a rolling pin to around $1/4$ inch thick.
Cut into shapes with a cutter.

Place onto the baking tray and place in the oven.
Cook for 15 minutes then turn the biscuits over. Cook for a further 15 minutes.

Turn the oven off and leave the biscuits in the oven until cold.
Store in the fridge in an airtight container.

These biscuits freeze well.
Makes about 70 little biscuits.

Di, a lovely old girl who enjoyed her twilight years with Fen Bank Greyhounds.

www.fenbankgreyhounds.co.uk/

Charlie's Country Crunch

Not a recipe for the faint hearted as this dough takes some kneading, but it makes loads of big biscuits and the dogs go mad for them.

INGREDIENTS

1 packet yeast
$1/4$ cup (50ml) warm water
$1/4$ teaspoon honey
2 salt free stock cubes
$1/2$ cup (50g) powdered skimmed milk
$2^1/4$ cups (450ml) cup boiling water
1 egg
$1/4$ cup (100g) honey
$1/4$ cup (50ml) vegetable oil
2 cups (300g) plain flour
5 cups (650g) wholemeal flour
1 cup (135g) wheat germ
2 cups (400g) bulgar wheat
1 extra beaten egg for brushing.

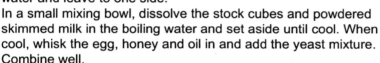

METHOD

Pre heat the oven to 180°C, gas mark 4.
Cover a baking tray with baking paper.

In a large bowl, dissolve the yeast and ¼ teaspoon of honey in the warm water and leave to one side.

In a small mixing bowl, dissolve the stock cubes and powdered skimmed milk in the boiling water and set aside until cool. When cool, whisk the egg, honey and oil in and add the yeast mixture. Combine well.

In a very large bowl: combine the flour, wheatgerm and bulgur wheat.

Make a well in the middle and add the wet ingredients. Stir with a spoon until the dough starts to stick together into one ball.

Divide the dough into two or three balls and turn them out in turn onto a floured worktop. Knead for a couple of minutes until smooth and no longer sticky. Roll it out to about ¼ inch thick then cut into biscuits using a cutter.

Place onto the baking tray and brush with the extra beaten egg.

If you have time, leave the biscuits for 15 minutes in a warm place to rise. If you are busy, you can cook them straight away.

Bake for 20 minutes then turn over, brush with egg and bake for another 25 minutes.

Makes 70–80 large sized biscuits.

My big fella Charlie – rehomed through a Retired Greyhound Trust kennels in Essex.

www.greyhoundhomer.org.uk/

Reuben's Raspberry & Blueberry Delights

These biscuits are a gorgeous pink colour due to the fruit and the dogs enjoy them.
Blueberries are said to help keep the old grey matter healthy too.

INGREDIENTS
1^1/$_2$ cups (195g) wholemeal flour
1^1/$_2$ cups (225g) plain flour
2 tablespoons wheatgerm
^{1}/$_2$ teaspoon ground cinnamon
^{1}/$_2$ cup (100ml) water
^{1}/$_4$ cup (80g) blueberries (fresh or frozen)
^{1}/$_4$ cup (80g) raspberries (fresh or frozen)
2 tablespoons honey
1 tablespoon safflower or olive oil
2 eggs
1 teaspoon vanilla essence
1 extra egg for washing (optional)

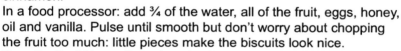

METHOD

Pre heat the oven to 180°C gas mark 4.
Cover a baking tray with baking paper.

In a large bowl, combine the flours, wheatgerm and cinnamon.

In a food processor: add ¾ of the water, all of the fruit, eggs, honey, oil and vanilla. Pulse until smooth but don't worry about chopping the fruit too much: little pieces make the biscuits look nice.

Pour the liquid ingredients into the flours and stir with a spoon until it all sticks into one ball of dough. You can add some of your reserved water if the dough is a little dry.

Turn the dough onto a floured worktop and kneed until smooth.

Roll out to ¼-½ inch thickness and cut with a cookie cutter.

Place the biscuits onto the baking tray.

You may choose to brush them with a beaten egg if you want them to be golden and glossy.

Cook for 20 minutes then carefully turn them all over. If you are going to egg wash: brush the new top side.

Cook for a further 20 minutes.

For crunchier biscuits, turn the oven off and leave the biscuits in the oven until cold.

Makes about 26 middle sized cookies.

If you only have one or the other of the berries they will turn out just fine too.

Reuben, a gorgeous Spanish galgo, rehomed by
www.greyhoundsinneed.co.uk/

Wilbour's Golden Wonders

Lovely golden biscuits, full of essential oils for a shiny coat.

INGREDIENTS
1 cup (125g) drained tinned peas and carrots
2 cups (260g) wholemeal flour
$^1/_2$ cup (100g) bulgar wheat
$^1/_2$ cup (50g) skimmed milk powder
6 tablespoons vegetable oil
1 beaten egg
$^1/_4$ cup (50ml) cold water

METHOD
Pre heat oven to 180ºC, gas mark 4.
Cover a baking tray with baking paper.

Using a hand blender or processor, puree the peas and carrots until smooth.

In a large mixing bowl, combine flours and skimmed milk powder.
Stir in the pea mixture, oil and egg.
Gradually add the water until the dough sticks together in one ball.

Turn out onto a floured worktop and knead for a couple of minutes until smooth.

Roll out with a rolling pin until between $^1/_4$-$^1/_2$ inch thick.
Cut out using cookie cutter and place on the baking tray.
Cook for 20 minutes, then turn over carefully.
Cook for up to another 25 minutes until the biscuits start to go golden.

Cool on a rack and store in an airtight container.
These biscuits freeze well.
Makes about 50 small biscuits.

COOK'S TIP
The longer you cook, the crunchier the biscuit and the longer they keep.

The gorgeous Wilbour enjoying his new home with his new friend. Wilbour rehomed by Erin Hounds ***www.erinhounds.co.uk***

Ginger's Gummy Bakes

Ideal for the dentally challenged dog!

INGREDIENTS
125g jar of baby food
$^1/_2$ cup (65g) wheatgerm
$^3/_4$ cup (60g) skimmed milk powder

METHOD
Pre heat the oven to 180°C gas mark 4.
Cover a baking tray with baking paper.

You can use any flavour baby food: but avoid any containing onion powder. Fish bake, sweet potato and the rice pudding with apple have been particularly popular.

Empty all the ingredients into a bowl and mix well with a spoon. Some baby foods are dryer than others, so you may wish to hold back a little of the milk powder until you have stirred the mixture a little.

The mixture should be sticky enough to mould into little balls.

Using a teaspoonful as a guide amount, shape into small balls and place onto the baking tray.
Each batch should make about 16 bites no bigger than ¾ of an inch.

Cook for 20-25 minutes or until starting to turn golden: cook for 30 minutes if you want dryer, crunchier treats, or just turn the oven off and leave the treats in there until cool.

Leave on a wire tray to cool.

These will need to be stored in a refrigerator.

COOK'S TIP
Friends who make these use them to stuff big Kong toys for hours of fun!

Ginger having a snooze with his cat friend Brian courtesy of Bridlington RGT. **bridlington.retiredgreyhounds.org** *Bridlington is just one of many Retired Greyhound Trust rehoming centres, see* **www.retiredgreyhounds.co.uk** *for your nearest branch.*

Remi's Rumpy Pumpkin

A firm favourite at Halloween made into fun scary bat and ghost shapes.

INGREDIENTS
1½ cups (195g) wholemeal flour
1 cup (100g) oats
2 teaspoons baking powder
1 teaspoon ground cinnamon
1 teaspoon ground ginger
3 tablespoons safflower or olive oil
½ cup (115g) tinned pumpkin
¼ cup (60g) unsalted peanut butter
½ cup (100ml) water

METHOD
Preheat the oven to 180°C gas mark 4.
Cover a baking tray with baking paper.

Place the flour, oats, baking powder, cinnamon and ginger in a bowl and mix well.

Make a well in the flour and stir the oil in until crumbly.

Add the pumpkin and peanut butter and stir until all combined.

Add the water and gently form into one ball of dough.

Turn out onto a floured worktop and knead until smooth.

Roll out to ½ inch thick and cut using a cookie cutter (Halloween shapes look great)

Place onto the baking tray and place into the oven.

Cook for 20 minutes, then turn the oven off and leave the biscuits until cool.

Makes about 35 small sized biscuits.

COOK'S TIP
If you cannot find tinned pumpkin – you can either cook your own, or replace with cooked sweet potato or squash. Just peel and chop your potato or squash, and cook in the microwave or a saucepan with a little water until soft. Drain and mash.

The lovely little Remi enjoying her new family life. Photo courtesy of Walthamstow Owners and Welfare Association.

www.wsretiredgreyhounds.co.uk

Booster's Berry & Turkey Cookies

Everyone loves these: use a Christmas tree shaped cutter and give them as presents. What could be better.

INGREDIENTS
225g turkey mince
2 cups (260g) wholemeal flour
$^{1}/_{2}$ cup (60g) wheat germ
1 egg beaten
(plus an extra egg for brushing – optional)
$^{1}/_{3}$ cup (60ml) olive oil
$^{1}/_{4}$ cup (25g) dried cranberries chopped finely in a blender

METHOD
Cook the turkey mince in a pan or microwave with a little water. This should take about 10 minutes at a low simmer. Allow to cool.

Pre heat oven to 180ºC, gas mark 4.
Cover a baking tray with baking paper.

In a large bowl, mix the flour, wheat germ, beaten egg, oil and cranberries.

Add the turkey mince but none of the juice yet.
Stir well and add a little of the turkey juice so that the mixture will stick as one ball of dough. This will probably be ½ cup (100ml)
Turn out onto a floured worktop or board and knead a little until smooth.
Roll out until about $^{1}/_{4}$-$^{1}/_{2}$ inch thick.
Cut out with a cookie cutter and place on the baking tray.
Brush with beaten egg if you choose to.
Cook in the oven for 25 minutes.
Turn each cookie over and brush with egg.
Cook for another 15 minutes, then turn the oven off.
Leave the biscuits in the oven until cool.

Makes about 24 large-sized biscuits.

COOK'S TIP
These freeze well.

Booster, a lovely sponsor dog courtesy of Wimbledon Greyhound Rescue.

www.hershamhounds.org

Katie's Cheese & Cranberry Christmas Biscuits

Light and golden with flecks of cranberry.
These look gorgeous in star shapes for Christmas but are great anytime of the year.

INGREDIENTS
2 cups (300g) plain flour
$^1/_3$ cup (60ml) olive oil
2 cups (200g) grated cheese
(use a mix of cheddar and parmesan if you wish)
$^1/_4$ cup (25g) dried cranberries chopped in a blender
$^1/_2$-$^3/_4$ cup (100-150ml) water
1 egg for glazing

METHOD
Pre heat oven to 180ºC, gas mark 4.
Cover a baking tray in baking paper.

Place all ingredients apart from the water in a large bowl and mix thoroughly.
Slowly add sufficient water until you can stick the dough into one ball.
Turn out onto a floured worktop and knead until smooth.

Roll out until $^1/_4$-$^1/_2$ inch thick and cut out shapes using a cookie cutter.
Transfer onto the baking tray.
Brush with egg and place in the oven.

Cook for 30-35 minutes or until they are just starting to turn golden.

Turn the oven off and leave the cookies in the oven until cool.

Makes 35 middle-sized biscuits.

The gorgeous Katy (on the right) enjoying a blast on the beach: courtesy of Dumfries & Cumbria Rescue.

www.dgrescue.org.uk

Frankie's Fish, Chip & Pea Biscotti

These are ideal for dogs with wheat and gluten allergies. This recipe makes a lot of biscotti – but they freeze well.

INGREDIENTS
1 cup (170g) potato flour
1 cup (150g) brown rice flour
$^1/_2$ cup (50g) oats
2 teaspoons baking powder
90g tin tuna or salmon, drained
2 tablespoons tinned peas
2 tablespoons oil (safflower or olive)
1 cup (200ml) cold water

METHOD
Pre heat oven to 180°C gas mark 4.
Cover a baking tray in baking paper.

Place all dry ingredients into a mixing bowl, stirring with a fork until mixed well.

In a separate bowl, mush the fish and peas well with a fork.
Add the fish and pea mixture and oil to the dry ingredients and stir well.
Make a well in the flour mixture and add 100ml of water in one go.
Mix with your hands until it is one ball of dough. Add more water if required until the will stays together.
Give it a good knead, then wrap in cling film and put in the fridge for $^{1}/_{2}$ an hour.

Take out of fridge and shape with your hands into a long square sausage about 3 inches wide and $^{3}/_{4}$ inch deep.
Slice with a knife into little biscuits about $^{3}/_{4}$ inch wide.
Place on the baking tray.

Cook for 30 minutes and then turn over. Cook for another 30-35 minutes until dry and firm to the touch, then turn the oven off and leave the biscuits in the oven until cold.
Remove them from the oven and place on a cooling rack.
These keep for ages as they are so dry, but keep them in an airtight box and cool.

Makes about 35 biscotti.

COOK'S TIP
They also freeze well.

Frankie, a lovely old boy courtesy, of Greyhound Rescue North East.

www.greyhoundrescue.net

Shinty's Salmon & Sunflower Cookies

Low in gluten but not in taste. High in all of the goodies needed for shiny coat.

INGREDIENTS
180g tin salmon complete with liquid
2 eggs
Pinch of parsley
$^1/_3$ cup (50g) sunflower hearts
$1^1/_2$ cups (240g) gluten free flour or
brown rice flour

Optional: 1 extra egg beaten for washing.

METHOD
Pre heat the oven to 180°C, gas mark 4.
Cover a baking tray with baking paper.

You can use red or pink salmon, red just makes a nicer coloured biscuit.
Mix all ingredients in a large bowl until you can make one lump of dough.
Add more flour if too wet and add a little water if too dry.

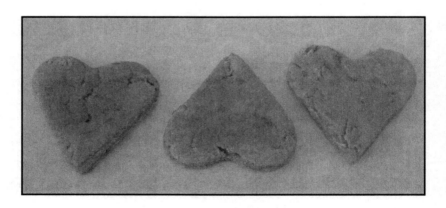

Roll out the dough to ½ inch thick (use plenty of flour on your worktop) and cut with a cookie cutter (preferably not too fancy as the seeds make it difficult to make complex shapes.)
If you wish, brush with the extra beaten egg to give colour and shine.
Place on a baking tray covered with greaseproof paper and cook for 25-30 minutes.

If brushing with egg, turn over after 20 minutes and brush the other side.
Makes about 35 middle-sized biscuits.

COOK'S TIP
Be aware that fish such as salmon can have a high fat content, so feed small portions. If looking for a lower fat fish, use tinned tuna. Drain off the liquid and use the tuna with water to wet the dough.

Shinty, a lovely sponsor dog in the Skye RGT rehoming centre.

www.rgtskye.co.uk/

Annie's Anti Gas Biscuits

Not the most attractive biscuit as they are grey, but effective nonetheless.

INGREDIENTS
2 cups (320g) gluten free flour of any type
1/4 cup (15g) of activated charcoal powder
(available from pet shops)
2 teaspoons baking powder (gluten free if you have it)
3 tablespoons olive oil
1/4 cup (25g) skimmed milk powder
1 teaspoon dried mint
1–11/4 cups (200–225ml) cold water

METHOD
Pre heat the oven to 180ºC, gas mark 4, and cover a baking tray with baking paper.

Place all of the dry ingredients in a bowl and mix well.
Add the oil and water and stir with a large spoon until it sticks into one ball of dough.

Press into one ball with your hands and turn out onto a worktop or board sprinkled with a little gluten free flour. Squeeze the dough into a long sausage, flattening a little with your hands. It can be any size but about 1 inch deep and about 3 inches wide is ideal.

Using a knife, slice into little slices about 1 inch thick like little biscotti biscuits.

Place carefully onto your baking tray and place into the oven. Cook for 25 minutes, then turn gently over. Cook for another 5-10 minutes then take out to cool.

Makes about 35 biscotti.

COOK'S TIP
You can make these with plain white flour: take out the baking powder, but they will contain gluten and the anti-gas effect will be reduced.

Annie, a sponsor dog at Hall Green RGT rehoming centre.

www.hallgreenrgt.co.uk

Loki's Low Cal Carrot Biscuits

Low in fat and calories, but dogs still love these.

INGREDIENTS
3¹/₂ cups (455g) wholemeal flour
1 cup (55g) wheat or oat bran
¹/₄ cup (25g) skimmed milk powder
¹/₂ cup (85g) grated carrots
¹/₂ ultra low salt stock cube
¹/₂ cup (100ml) warm water
¹/₂ cup (150g) apple sauce
2 egg whites

METHOD
Pre heat the oven to 180°C gas mark 4.
Cover a baking tray in baking paper.

In a large bowl, combine the flour, bran and milk powder.

In a second bowl, dissolve the half stock cube in the warm water.
In a food processor or by hand, grate the carrots then add to the
stock. Add the apple sauce and egg whites and mix well.
Add the liquid to the flours and stir with a large spoon until the
dough sticks together in one ball.

Turn out onto a floured worktop and knead for a minute or two until
smooth.

Roll out to $^1/_4$-$^1/_2$ inch thickness and cut with a cookie cutter.
Place onto the baking tray.

Cook for 15 minutes then turn over and cook for another 15 minutes.
For crunchier biscuits, turn the oven off and leave the biscuits in the
oven until cold.

Makes 32 middle-sized biscuits.

Loki wowing his fans at a local dog show.
Rehomed through Northern Greyhound
Rescue.

www.northerngreyhoundrescue.org.uk/

Whisper's Waist Watcher Cheese Biscuits

A nice alternative to high fat cheese biscuits.

INGREDIENTS
1¹/₂ cups (195g) wholemeal flour
¹/₃ cup (35g) oats
¹/₃ cup (90g) tub of non-fat cream cheese
  (Quark or similar)
¹/₃ cup (100g) apple sauce
¹/₂ cup (100ml) water

METHOD
Pre heat the oven to 180°C, gas mark 4.
Cover a baking tray in baking paper.

Combine the flour and oatmeal in a large bowl.
Place the cream cheese, apple sauce and water in a food processor and blend until smooth – or beat by hand with a whisk.
Pour the apple mixture into the dry ingredients and stir until one ball of dough forms. Add more water or flour to ensure that it is not too sticky or dry.

Turn out onto a floured worktop and knead until smooth.
Roll out to $^1/_4$-$^1/_2$ inch thick and cut into shapes using a cookie cutter.
Place onto the baking tray.

Cook for 20–30 minutes depending upon the thickness, then turn onto a wire rack to cool.

You can also turn the oven off and leave the biscuits to cool if you want a crunchier texture.

These biscuits should be stored in the fridge in an airtight container.

Makes about 24 middle-sized biscuits.

COOK'S TIP
If you do not have 'no fat' cream cheese, look out for the very low fat cheese spreads.

Whisper, a lovely sponsor girlie living in Cork courtesy of
www.dogactionwelfaregroup.ie/index.html

Nubi's Nobbly Pumpkin Drops

Nice alternative to make if you can't roll out dough or don't have a cutter.

INGREDIENTS
1^1/$_2$ cups (195g) wholemeal flour
^{1}/$_2$ teaspoon ground cinnamon
^{1}/$_2$ teaspoon ground ginger
3 tablespoons apple sauce
2 egg whites
^{1}/$_2$ cup (115g) tinned or cooked pumpkin
1 tablespoon honey
^{1}/$_4$-^{1}/$_2$ cup (50-100ml) water

METHOD
Preheat the oven to 200°C: gas mark 6.

Combine all ingredients except the water in a large bowl and stir with a large spoon.
Add the water slowly to make the dough, a little sloppy like a cookie

dough. It should drop off the spoon with a shake. You may need to use all of the water. If your dough is firm your cookies will be higher – the wetter the mixture, the flatter your biscuits. Either way, they will be just fine.

Cover a baking tray with a greased baking sheet and, using a teaspoon, drop the cookie dough onto the sheet, 1 inch apart. Cook in the oven for 15-20 minutes, then turn the oven off and leave the cookies until cool.

Not the prettiest of treats as far as the eye goes, but the taste testers didn't seem to notice!
Makes about 26 drop cookies.
Store these in the refrigerator.

COOK'S TIP
If you cannot get pumpkin, you can use cooked sweet potato or butternut squash instead.

Nubi, Kent Greyhound Rescue's first officially rehomed hound, snuggling with the family cat.

www.kentgreyhoundrescue.co.uk/

Sophie's Ultra-low Protein Sweet Potato

An ideal treat for dogs with kidney or liver problems as there is very little protein in them.

INGREDIENTS
1 medium sweet potato (peeled weight 150g)
2 cups (330g) brown rice flour
$^{1}/_{2}$ ultra low salt stock cube
dissolved into 1 cup (200ml) hot water

METHOD
Pre heat oven to 180°C gas mark 4.
Cover a baking tray with baking paper.

Peel and cook the potato in water, simmering for about 15 minutes.
Leave to cool then strain and mash. Reserve the liquid.

Place in a bowl then add the flour.

Stir the stock cube liquid in, and add as much of the potato cooking water as you need to get it to stick into one ball of dough (about 100–150ml).

Flour a worktop well with rice flour and turn your dough out. Knead well with your hands until well blended then press to about $^1/_2$-$^3/_4$ inch thick with your hands.

Cut with a cookie cutter and place carefully onto your baking tray.

Cook in the oven 25 minutes or until starting to turn golden.

Makes about 16 middle-sized biscuits.

Sophie enjoyed her twilight time with Greyhound Rescue North Yorkshire.

www.greyhoundrescue-yorkshire.co.uk

Gemini Ginger Cookies

Ginger is well known for its tummy settling properties – so these may just help on those little trips in the car.

INGREDIENTS
2 cups (330g) brown rice flour
$^1/_2$ cup (50g) skimmed milk powder
1 tablespoon grated fresh ginger
$1^1/_4$ cups (225ml) water

METHOD
Pre heat the oven to 180°C gas mark 4.
Cover a large baking tray with baking paper.

In a large bowl add the flour, milk powder and ginger and mix well.
Add the water slowly and mix with a large spoon.
Use your hands to form the dough into one ball.

Remember that this is gluten low and will not be elastic.

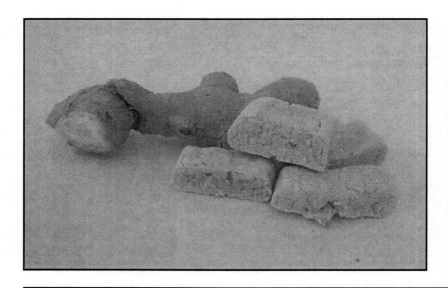

Turn out onto a floured worktop and, using your hands, shape it into a long square sausage. This should be about 3 inches wide and up to 1 inch thick.

Using a knife, cut into slices about 1 inch thick.
Lift carefully onto your baking tray.

Cook in the oven for 25 minutes then turn the oven off.
Take the biscuits out once cooled.

Makes about 50 little biscotti.

COOK'S TIP
If you don't have fresh ginger you can substitute 1 heaped teaspoon of dried ginger.

Piper waiting for his forever sofa at Gemini Kennels, Essex.

www.geminikennels.info/

Chelsea's Celebration Cake

Simply the best liver birthday cake – ever!

INGREDIENTS
1 cup (130g) wholemeal flour
$^1/_2$ cup (30g) wheat or oat bran
500g liver (preferably lamb but any will do)
2 medium carrots
$^1/_2$ cup (150g) apple sauce
$^1/_4$ cup (50ml) olive oil
1 egg

Frosting/filling
Small pot of cottage cheese

METHOD
Pre heat the oven to 180°C, gas mark 4.
Lightly grease an 8$^1/_2$ inch round cake tin and place a little baking paper in the bottom.

Cook the liver in a pan with a little water until done. Snip it up with scissors to speed up cooking. Leave to cool: then puree in a food processor with a small amount of the liquid.

In a large bowl, combine the flour and bran. Tip ¾ of the liver mixture in and stir well.
Chop or grate the carrots in a food processor and add the apple sauce, olive oil and egg. Mix thoroughly.

Add this to the flour and liver mixture and stir well. If too dry, add a little of the liver cooking liquid. The mixture should be sticky and not too liquid.
Spoon into the cake tin, filling it right to the brim. Place in the oven for 60-80 minutes.
Turn onto a wire rack once cool.

To ice: combine the reserved liver puree with the cottage cheese and spread over the cake.

COOK'S TIP
If you wish: double this recipe and make two cakes in two tins. Use the cottage cheese/liver mixture as a filling between the two and cover the top of the cake with light cream cheese. Why not decorate with heart shaped mini biscuits?

*Chelsea at the grand old age of 13 years, enjoying her birthday cake. Thanks to Chelsea, we now have **www.Greyhoundwalks.co.uk** raising awareness of the breed.*

Sasha's Sardine Sponge Cake

A firm favourite with everyone who tries it. A rustic looking fishy sponge cake.

INGREDIENTS
1 cup (170g) plain flour
1 tablespoon of baking powder.
2 large eggs
1 425g tin of sardines or pilchards in tomato sauce.

METHOD
Pre heat the oven to 180°C gas mark 4.
Lightly grease an 8 inch sponge tin and line the bottom with baking paper.

Sieve the flour and baking powder into a large mixing bowl.
Add the two eggs and all of the fish, but reserve the sauce, and mix well with a fork until smooth.

Tip the mixture into the cake tin – it should be about $^3/_4$ full and smooth the top flat.
Place in the oven and cook for 25-30 minutes.
Turn out once cool.

COOK'S TIP
This cake does not keep long, only a few days in the refrigerator; but does freeze well.

You can spread cottage cheese or low fat cream cheese over the top to make it extra special.

You can even use a little of the leftover tomato sauce to colour and flavour the cheese if your dogs like it. Mine LOVE it.

The lovely Sasha enjoying her birthday cake: and not really wanting to share! Sponsor girlie from ***www.greyhoundgap.org.uk/***

Kate's Carrot Cup Cakes

A lower calorie option. Scrummy nonetheless!

INGREDIENTS
1 cup (220g) apple sauce
2 (180g) carrots
2 tablespoons honey
2¹/₄ cup (450ml) cold water
¹/₄ teaspoon vanilla essence
1 egg
4 cups (600g) wholemeal flour
1 tablespoon baking powder
¹/₂ teaspoon cinnamon

METHOD
Preheat the oven to 180°C gas mark 4.
Lightly grease a muffin tray – I use a large muffin tray, but you can use small ones.

Top: Woody enjoys Barley jumping

Below: Reuben's Raspberry and Blueberry Delights

Top: Gracie enjoys a snooze

Right: Kate's Carrot Cup Cakes

Below: Wilbour's Golden Wonders

Above: Di Loves Liver Biscuits

Below: Grendel makes himself comfortable

Above: Tia, Ruby and Charlie – happy family

Right: Chester's Cheesy Chomps

Below: Poppy's Sweet Potato and Carrot

Main picture: Lady enjoys a jog in the sunshine

Inset: Wagger's Wild for Casserole

Right: Patience's Peanut Butter and Banana Bones

Below: Mo insists on being first!

Above: Nubi snuggles
with the cat

Left: Chelsea's
Celebration Cake

Left: Malarky's Minty
Mouthfuls

Left: Lady's Lovely Lamb Meatloaf

Below: Booster's Berry and Turkey Cookie

Below: Hound taste testers give their approval

Grate or chop the carrots in a food processor.

Combine the carrots, honey, water and vanilla essence in a bowl.
In a separate bowl, mix the flour, baking powder and cinnamon.
Pour the carrot mixture into the flour and stir gently with a spoon
until well blended.

Scoop the mixture into the muffin tin – filling each cup to about ¾
full.

Cook in the oven for 45-55 minutes. Test with a skewer or sharp
knife, it should come out of the centre dry when you test them.

COOK'S TIP
Reduce the cooking time by about 10 minutes if using small muffin
trays.

The gorgeous Kate, rehomed by
www.kerrygreyhounds.co.uk
Based in Kerry and Norfolk, England.

Winnie's Apple & Cheddar Muffins

These are so nice, I eat them myself!

INGREDIENTS
1 cup (155g) plain white flour
½ cup (90g) wholemeal flour
¼ cup (25g) oat or wheat bran
1 level tablespoon baking powder
½ cup (100g) of yoghurt
   (or two mini pots of fromage frais)
½ cup (100ml) cold water
¼ cup (50ml) vegetable oil
2 tablespoons honey
2 large eggs
1 large apple, cored, peeled and chopped
1 cup (100g) grated or chopped cheddar cheese

METHOD
Preheat the oven to 190°C gas 5.

Grease a muffin tray, or line with paper muffin cups if you prefer (if using a silicon tray – you don't need to do anything!)

In a large bowl mix the flours, bran and baking powder.

In a second bowl, whisk the yogurt, water, oil, honey and eggs. Then stir the cheese and apples into your liquid.

Gently stir the liquid into your flour until combined.
Spoon into the muffin tin, filling each one to about $3/4$ full.
Place into the oven and cook for 20-25 minutes until you can insert a knife into them and it comes out clean.
Leave to cool then remove from the tray.

COOK'S TIP
If you don't have a muffin tin you can make this in a normal sponge cake tin, an $8^1/2$ inch tin will do. You will probably need to increase the cooking time by 10 minutes or so and perhaps turn the oven down to 180°C for the last 10 minutes if it is getting a wee bit too brown.

Winnie, a rather lovely girlie from Swiss Valley Rescue: a fully qualified PAT dog.

www.freewebs.com/ swissvalleygreyhoundrescue

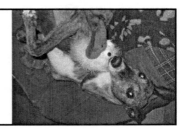

Wagger's Wild for Casserole

Fun but healthy lunch option.

INGREDIENTS
1 cup (200g) white rice
1 tablespoon wild rice
1 cup in total (100g) frozen peas, carrots and sweetcorn
1 cup (160g) liver, hearts, rabbit, chicken, venison, mutton or turkey
1 salt-free stock cube

METHOD
Cook whatever meat and offal you choose to add in a large sauce pan (preferably an old one!) with a salt-free stock cube and plenty of water.

To reduce the cooking time, snip the meat into small pieces using scissors.

When cooked through, drain, remove any bones, reserve the water, and leave to cool.

Measure one cup of white rice (plus 1 tablespoon of wild rice, optional) and cook as per the instructions on the packet. Cook using the drained meat liquid instead of plain water, however, then leave to cool. Cook whichever vegetables you choose to add (I think carrots, peas, green beans and sweetcorn looks great) and leave to cool.

When all the ingredients are cold: mix together the rice, meat and vegetables in a large bowl and serve.

COOK'S TIP
Why not try this for a doggie get together? I prepare this for fund raising events, and have a dining table for eat in, or take away containers for doggies who eat later.

1 cup of each ingredient when cooked and combined gives a soup ladle of dinner for 4-5 large hounds.
I just multiply up for more servings. Why not add a Charlie's Country Crunch on the side?

Wagger, my long suffering taste –tester: not at all impressed at wearing a bib and being dragged from his blanket for a photo shoot!

Doggie dinners being served at a garden party to raise funds for Essex and Suffolk greyhounds.

Lady's Lamb Pie

Doggy version of shepherds pie!

INGREDIENTS
500 gram pack of mince: preferably lamb but turkey will also do.
$^1/_2$ salt free stock cube
2 cups (400ml) water
Teaspoon dried mint (optional)
1 cup tinned or frozen vegetables (peas, carrots, sweetcorn)
250g potato (medium sized)
1 cup (155g) of plain flour
1 egg
1 teaspoon baking powder
1 tablespoon oil
1 tablespoon molasses (or honey)
$^1/_4$ cup(25g) grated cheese: cheddar or parmesan or a mixture of both.

METHOD
Preheat the oven to 180ºC gas mark 4.

Place your lamb, stock cube, mint and water in a saucepan and bring to the boil. Simmer gently for about 5 minutes until cooked. (This also microwaves nicely.) Leave to cool.

Cook your vegetables as per instructions on them and leave to cool. Peel, cook and mash your potato – don't forget, don't use salt during the cooking of either your vegetables or potatoes. Leave to cool.

In a dish suitable for the oven (a small lasagne dish will do nicely), add the lamb mince, some of the juice, and the vegetables. Stir and press down a little – it should be wet but not too sloppy or it will boil over the topping when cooking.

In a large bowl, place your mashed potatoes, the eggs, flour, baking powder, oil and molasses and stir well.
If the mixture is very stiff, you can trickle in a little of your reserved lamb liquid. It should be like firm mashed potato but spreadable.
Spread this potato mixture onto your lamb.
Sprinkle with grated cheese and cook in the oven for 25-30 minutes until the cheese is nicely toasted.

COOK'S TIP
Serve when cold with some of the lamb stock as gravy if you like. This freezes well.

The lovely Lady, permanent resident of
www.harlowhounds.org

Lady's Lovely Lamb Meatloaf

Always tempts a fussy eater and loved by all.

INGREDIENTS
1 cup (100g) tinned or frozen carrots grated or chopped
1 cup (100g) peas tinned or frozen
500g minced lamb
1¹/₂ cups (150g) oats
2 eggs, beaten
1 teaspoon dried mint
¹/₂ cup (40g) grated parmesan
2 slices granary bread (optional)

METHOD
Pre heat oven to 180°C gas mark 4.
Grease a loaf tin (or better still obtain a silicon one as you do not have to grease or line them).

If you have the granary bread, remove the crusts and line the base of the meat loaf tin.

Place all of your ingredients in a large mixing bowl and mush together well with your hands.
When well blended, place into the meatloaf tin and firm gently to expel any large gaps.
Place into the centre of the oven and cook for $1^1/_2$ hours.

Leave to cool then turn out and cut into slices.

COOK'S TIP
This meat loaf freezes well, why not freeze slices in bags in daily sized portions?

Lady, a scrummy old lady courtesy of
www.greyhoundrescuewales.co.uk

Tinker's Turkey Gobble

Irresistible to every dog who tries it.
Particularly useful for little people who are picky eaters or those with delicate tummies.

INGREDIENTS
500g Turkey mince
2 cups (200g) oats
2 eggs
$^{1}/_{2}$ cup (40g) grated parmesan cheese
2 slices of granary bread (optional)

METHOD
Pre heat oven to 180 C, gas mark 4.

Grease a loaf tin (or better still acquire a silicon one: they're fantastic and you don't have to grease or line them).

Place all the ingredients, except the bread, into a mixing bowl and mix with your hands until all blended nicely.

To give the top of the loaf a nice finish, remove the crusts from your granary bread and place in the bottom of the tin.
Tip your mince into the tin, and firm down with your fingers – but not too hard.

Place in the centre of the oven and cook 45 minutes to 1 hour.
To check if it's done, insert a knife into the centre and it should come out dry and clean.

When cool, turn out of the tin, slice and serve.

COOK'S TIP
Like the lamb meatloaf, why not cut into slices and freeze in small portions?

Tinker courtesy of
www.tiagreyhounds.org.uk

Nobby's Nuts for Liver Cake

INGREDIENTS
250g liver
1¹/₂ cups (250g) self raising flour
2 eggs
Milk

METHOD
Pre heat oven to 180°C, gas mark 4.

In a blender, puree the liver and eggs.
Put the flour in a bowl and stir in the liver mixture. Add sufficient milk to make a 'spongy' texture.

Pour into a baking tray lined with foil and cook for 50-60 minutes.

Turn out when cold and cut into small cubes: this makes great training titbits.

For a more solid, less crumbly cake – use plain flour.

Freeze in small bags and thaw when you need it.

Handsome Nobby courtesy of
www.greyhounds4u.co.uk/

Ben Bounces for Chicken Cake

A handy recipe when you have some left over chicken and excellent for training as not as greasy on the hands. Makes a very dense heavy slab.

INGREDIENTS
1 cup (160g) cooked chicken
$^1/_2$ a salt-free stock cube
3$^1/_4$ cups (650ml) warm water
2 large eggs
2 cups (330g) brown rice flour
3 cups (390g) wholemeal flour

METHOD
Pre heat the oven to 180°C, gas mark 4 and grease a shallow cake tin or baking tray.

Add the water to the stock cube and stir until dissolved.

Place the chicken, stock and eggs in a food processor and pulse until a smooth puree.

Add the flours and pulse until it sticks into one ball of dough. If your eggs are a little small, you can add up to another 100ml of water: you are looking for a sloppy dough like porridge.

Pour into the greased pan and place in the oven for 20 minutes, or until the dough starts to come away from the sides of the tray.
It will be very dense and solid, not like a sponge cake in any way.
Turn out onto a wire tray when cool, then cut into squares.

Freezes well but will also keep in the fridge in an airtight container for several days.

COOK'S TIP
This makes great dog training treats as it is not as rich as the liver cake.
If your dog has a problem with chicken, substitute turkey slices.

Ben and Honey snuggle with the family cat. Happily rehomed by Romford Greyhound Owners Trust for Retired Greyhounds.
www.Rgoa.co.uk/

Timmy's Tasty Tuna Training Bits

Makes a dense slab which chops into nice cubes for training. Lighter on the tummy than liver training cake – and less fattening than lumps of cheese.

INGREDIENTS
2 200g cans of tuna in water
2 eggs
1¹/₂ cups (240g) brown rice flour
Grated parmesan cheese – optional

METHOD
Preheat the oven to 180°C gas mark 4.

Empty the tins of tuna into a bowl, complete with liquid.
Mash well with a fork.

Add the eggs and flour and mash together well.
The consistency should be a firm cake mixture. If a little dry, sprinkle some water in.

Spread the mixture into a baking tray or square cake pan.
Sprinkle with the grated parmesan, if you choose.

Cook in the oven for 15 minutes until firm all over.

Turn out once cool and chop into small cubes.

COOK'S TIP
This freezes well.

Timmy, who enjoyed his twilight time at Clarks Farm as a sponsor dog.
www.clarksfarmgreyhounds.ik.com

Jack's Liver Jerky

Why buy it when it is so easy to make?

INGREDIENTS
500g of liver
Water

METHOD
Pre heat the oven to 160°C gas mark 3c, and cover a baking tray with foil.

Snip the liver into treat size pieces with scissors and place into a saucepan.
Cover with water and bring to the boil.
Reduce the heat and simmer, stirring occasionally for 5 minutes.

Drain and place onto your baking tray then put in the oven.
Cook for 1 hour then turn them over.
Cook for another 45 minutes. Leave out to cool.

It's probably best to cook this when you are going out! It's a bit
pongy to say the least, but it makes excellent, irresistible treats.

COOK'S TIP
Keep the water left over from the recipe as it is excellent for stock. It
can be used for the recipes in this book or just poured over your
hound's dinner biscuits. It can be frozen for several months and
thawed when needed.

*Jack, the handsome sponsor dog
from Greyhound & Lurcher
Welfare Rescue.*

www.glwr.org.uk/

APPLE SAUCE
Apple sauce not only provides flavour, but it is a good substitute for oil if you want to cut down the fat in your dog's diet.

1 kilo of cooking apples makes almost 4 cups of apple sauce. Simply peel, chop, add a little water and cook in the microwave or a saucepan for 12 minutes. Then mash or puree with a processor.

Don't add any lemon juice as you would if making this for humans (to prevent it from going brown), as this is for dogs. Citrus is not good for dogs and they will not mind brown apple sauce.

This freezes well, so make up a batch ready for your baking.

If you buy ready made, try to buy it with no sugar and additives added.

BABY FOODS
Most baby foods are organic and have no salt/little sugar.

They make excellent flavourings for doggie foods. Avoid any types that have onion powder or citrus.

BANANAS
Bananas are fat-free, contain vitamins, fibre and taste great.
Dogs love them.

BRAN
Bran is the outside hull of wheat or oats.
This is very high in fibre, which can help with impacted anal glands.

CAROB
Similar in taste to cocoa, carob does not contain caffeine and is safe for dogs.

Available in health food shops in powdered form.

CARROTS
Carrots are an excellent source of antioxidant compounds and carotenes.

They help protect the body against cardiovascular disease and cancer. They also promote good vision, especially night vision.

CHEESE
Cheese adds flavour and aroma to recipes and it also provides protein and calcium.

Most dogs can enjoy cheese in small amounts, but some suffer from lactose intolerance as they get older. This can be seen as excessive gas, stomach ache and diarrhoea. You can always use sheep or goats cheese as this may not cause such reactions.

When grating cheese for cooking, why not grate a whole block and freeze in small bags? It keeps for three months.

CORNMEAL
In the UK, you can purchase this under the name of maize meal from health food shops. You can also use chick pea flour. It is a non-wheat, gluten-free flour, and very protein rich. If your dog is sensitive, substitute wholemeal flour or bran.

COUSCOUS
This is a coarsely ground semolina pasta.

It can be used in the place of rice for a quick, easy to digest meal for dogs.

CRANBERRIES
Great for urinary health for both dogs and humans and can help to prevent bladder infections. Don't overdo the portions, however, as they can be quite acidic. Dried cranberries are fine for these recipes, but be aware that some may have been sweetened, so cut down the portions in the recipes.

EGGS
Eggs not only hold a dough together, but they add protein and fat. The recipes in this book use large eggs.

If you want to cut down the fat in the biscuits, use two egg whites in the place of one egg.

FENNEL SEEDS
These can be added to any of the recipes in this book. They add a pleasant aniseed flavour and can aid digestion.

FISH
Most dogs love fish and they are great for flavouring biscuits. When buying tinned salmon and tuna, buy the cheapest as it will contain more skin and bones and this will give your dog more calcium (the soft bones in salmon and tuna are quite safe).

Be aware that fish such as salmon can have a high fat content, so feed small portions. If looking for a lower fat fish, use tuna.
It is important to note that some fish can be harmful to dogs when eaten raw. Don't take the risk, if buying raw fish; cook it and triple check for bones, as the bones in cod, etc., are very sharp.

Pet shops often sell blocks of frozen fish, which is excellent. Why not make a fish version of the lamb pie from this book for a nice change?

GARLIC
Garlic is said to be excellent for blood and skin conditions as well as for repelling fleas.

There are also reports, however that show that it can cause problems in dogs if fed at a too high a dose. It is part of the onion family after all – and we do not feed onions to our dogs.

Having weighed all of the information, I decided not to include garlic in my recipes. The choice, however, is yours.

Should you wish to feed garlic, you can add a small amount to the savoury recipes in this book.

GINGER
This can be grated into the recipes in small amounts.

It gives a nice spicy, lemony flavour, but is well known for its stomach-settling qualities. Consider having some of the ginger goodies ready made for car journeys if your doggie gets a little travel sick.

HONEY
Some dogs have a real sweet tooth and honey is a healthy source of natural sugar.

If a recipe needs honey and oil, measure the oil first and it will stop the honey sticking to the cup.

It is said to aid with allergies, but to benefit: you need to purchase the honey from your local area. Check out your local farmers' market, as these will also be fresh and won't contain any unwanted 'extras'.

LIVER AND OFFAL
All dogs love liver and offal. You can use any type, but pork is often the cheapest. I prefer lamb, however. Whenever possible, do buy organic liver, as this is the organ that processes toxins. I look out for it reduced and place it straight in the freezer ready for when I need it.

MILK
If your dog is dairy or milk sensitive: replace the milk with rice or soy milk.

Powdered skimmed milk is used in this book as it adds good flavour. You can also sprinkle it on top of your biscuits before cooking to give them a crunchy topping.

MINT
Mint aids digestion and is a natural breath freshener.

MOLASSES
Another healthy sweetener and adds a great dark taste to the recipes. Try to use Blackstrap molasses if you can get it, this has more minerals and is less sweet.

OATS
Oats add a rustic texture to recipes. Avoid 'quick cook oats' as they may have been treated and contain ingredients other than oats.

Lots of supermarkets sell a budget range of oats, which are excellent but are just finer than the more expensive brands.

OILS
Like humans, dogs need oils and fats in their diet, within reasonable limits.

Good fats are found in ingredients like peanut oil and vegetable oils.

Bad 'cholesterol' fats are found in animal meats and processed foods.

OLIVE OIL
Cold pressed olive oil is the best to use for both you and your dogs. Oil of this type has been extracted without the use of chemicals.

SAFFLOWER AND SUNFLOWER OILS
More and more of our supermarkets are now stocking these more unusual types of oils.

These oils contain Omega 6 fatty acids which are important to your dog's health. Again, try to get cold pressed oils.

FISH OILS
Oils such as cod liver oil and fish oil can be used in these recipes. They are excellent for a healthy coat and skin.

PEANUT BUTTER
Try to buy the type with no salt or sugar added: most supermarkets now stock this. Health food shops sell a brand which is just crushed nuts. It a little expensive but you will make loads of biscuits from one tub and it keeps for ages in the fridge.

Peanut butter gives flavour and fibre: its calories are converted into pure energy – good biscuits to take on a long day out with your dogs.

PUMPKIN
This is very popular in American doggie cookbooks. I have found this in our supermarkets in tins.

It is very low in calories and high in fibre, so is great for dog biscuits. You can always substitute sweet potato or a butternut squash, but do try to grab some pumpkin if you see it.

To cook pumpkin or squash, cut it in half, scoop out the seeds and discard them. Remove the flesh and chop into cubes. Cook in water until soft. It should take about 10 minutes in the microwave or a pan with just a little water.

RABBIT
If you can source it, get some.

Low in fat, organic and free range: it is healthy for both humans and dogs.

When using, double check for small splintery bones in the meat. Just cook on the stove in a large pan with a low salt stock cube until falling apart, this makes it easier to de-bone. Freezes well ready for use – and remember to save your stock for the biscuit recipes!

RICE, SOY AND POTATO FLOUR
Some dogs have allergies or an intolerance to the gluten found in wheat flours. These flours do not contain gluten, but can be tricky to work with. Gluten gives dough 'elasticity', and gluten free recipes can crumble. Try to make your dough a little wetter and perhaps press into a log and chop into round biscuits rather than use cutters. Brown rice flour contains the wholegrain and is more nutritious but less easily digested than white rice flour.

STOCK
Many of us do not have the time to boil bones and make stock, but so many stock cubes available are laced with lots of salt.

Many supermarkets and all health food shops stock very low salt stock cubes. They are excellent for biscuits and contain so little salt as to not affect your hound.

Alternatively, you can also cook a portion of liver or hearts in water. Your dog will love to eat the meat for you, and you get to keep and freeze the liquid for when it is needed.

VENISON
More readily available now in supermarkets, but also look out for venison at local farmers' markets or country estates. Venison is high in protein but low in saturated fat and contains good levels of iron. It is lower in fat and calories than beef. It is also organic and, more often than not, free range.

VEGETABLES
An essential source of fibre and vitamins, many vegetables can be fed cooked or raw.

Carrots, peas, green beans, sweetcorn, spinach and sweet potato can all be given.

Remember if feeding from a tin to check out salt levels. Frozen vegetables can often be best as they have nothing added, and you can also use the quantity you need without waste.

YOGHURT AND FROMAGE FRAIS
Dogs love a yoghurt or fromage frais, just avoid ones with sweeteners and citrus fruit.

I usually look out for organic children's yoghurts when they are on special offer in the supermarket. My boys have a couple each week and really enjoy them.

WHEAT GERM
This is loaded with vitamin E for a healthy coat and skin.

WHOLEMEAL FLOUR
This type of flour includes the germ and bran of the wheat. It is more nutritious than white flour and gives recipes a firmer texture and stronger taste.

Gives dough 'elasticity' and makes it easy to work with.

Interesting facts

Omega 6 and Omega 3, found in wholegrains and cereals, vegetables and vegetable oils, eggs, poultry and fish such as salmon are excellent for good health.

They can reduce inflammations associated with skin allergies, arthritis and intestinal disorders.

Iron, calcium and phosphorus are three of the most important minerals in your dog's diet. Meat and liver are rich in iron, as are egg yolks and dark green vegetables.

Calcium is found in hard cheeses, leafy greens and small fish such as sardines.

Blueberries are packed with a number of nutrients like vitamins C and E and have very few calories. They also contain antioxidants called anthocyanidins and help neutralise the tissues that potentially cause heart disease, peptic ulcers, cataracts and glaucoma. They are also said to protect the brain from age-related conditions such as dementia and Alzeimers disease.

Biscotti are crisp Italian cookies, formed into long slabs and cut into wedges. They are cooked until they are dry and crisp. They are ideal for gluten-free recipes as you do not need to roll the dough, you can just shape it with your hands.

Being baked until crispy dry means that they can be stored for ages.

Apple sauce can be substituted for the oil within a recipe if you are looking to reduce the fat and calorie content in your dog's diet. Make your own sauce: it is quick, cheap and you know that there will be no hidden sugar or preservatives.

Foods to Avoid

ALCOHOL
I know that some dogs love to pinch a bit of beer: but alcohol isn't good for dogs and can do quite a lot of harm even in small quantities.

CAFFEINE
Caffeine is found in coffee, tea, chocolate and certain fizzy drinks. It is toxic to dogs and can affect their hearts and nervous system.

CHOCOLATE
Chocolate contains theobromine and caffeine. In dogs this can increase the heart rate, cause difficulty breathing, vomiting, diarrhoea and excessive urination.

It can lead to seizures and even death.

CITRUS
Lemons and limes are toxic to dogs when ingested. They can cause vomiting, drooling and trembling.

Be aware that insecticidal sprays, insect repellents and household fragrances can all contain citrus extracts.

GRAPES AND RAISINS
These contain toxins that can affect the kidneys and liver. Some dogs are more susceptible than others.

MACADAMIA NUTS
These can affect the muscular system as well as digestive and nervous systems.

MSG
This is a common food 'flavour enhancer' added to many human foods.

Allergic reactions in humans and dogs may include headaches, tingling, numbness and, in extreme cases, difficulty breathing.

MUSHROOMS

Mushrooms contain various toxins that can affect the nervous system, causing vomiting and diarrhoea.

ONIONS

Although onions come from the same family as garlic, they are harmful to dogs.

They can cause abnormalities in red blood cells resulting in anaemia